Focus On Minerals

By Jerry Wermund

Illustrated by Tony Sansevero

Rockon Publishing

Focus On Minerals

First Edition 2007
Text Copyright© by Jerry Wermund
Illustrations Copyright© by Tony Sansevero
Photographs Copyright© by Jerry Wermund
Book Design by Tim Wermund

Copyright© Rockon Publishing
210 Hy Road, Buda , Texas 78610

ISBN 0-9726255-2-6

Printed in China through Creative Printing USA

Keywords = Children's Nonfiction. Geology [1. Rock Names, 2. History,
3. Social Use, 4. Games]. Children's Poetry.

DEDICATION AND ACKNOWLEDGEMENTS

To Dirk and Ed Wermund
To Giana Sansevero

Thank you to our models for our illustrations:
Jack Gillies, John Graham Shearer, Johnee Wolter,
Jeffrey and Sarah Littlefield, Theron Kassens, Josh Christman,
Ethan Mccully, Reilly and Peyton Havranek, Denali Kervella and Morgan Eddolls

Thank you to the Texas Memorial Museum for the loan of mineral specimens at
their Invertebrate Paleontology Laboratory.

Thank you to Allan Standen, gemologist and mineralogist, for permitting
photography of minerals in his Private Collection.

Thank you to Allan Standen, Betty X. Davis, Jane Peddicord and
Maryanne Simmons for peer review and editorial help.

Thank you to Doris Jean Laird for final edit.

Not animal;   **not vegetable;**   **must be mineral.**

Minerals are non-living hard materials composed of atoms joining together. You can tell minerals apart based on their physical properties. The properties include crystal structure (shape), color, streak (color of powdered mineral), luster (appearance in reflected light), hardness, cleavage (breakage along flat surfaces) and weight (compared to weight of water).

HOW MINERALS ARE NAMED

What's in a mineral name?
a place – Franklinite from
Franklin, New Jersey.
a property –
Magnetite from
magnetism.
an old language –
Argentite from argyros,
ancient Greek for silver.
a person –
Alexandrite
from Alexander.

Mineralogists, who find a new mineral, sometimes name the mineral after a famous friend. If you find a new mineral, you can name it by adding "ite" to you name. If your name is Johnson the new mineral could be "Johnsonite."

CRYSTAL STRUCTURE

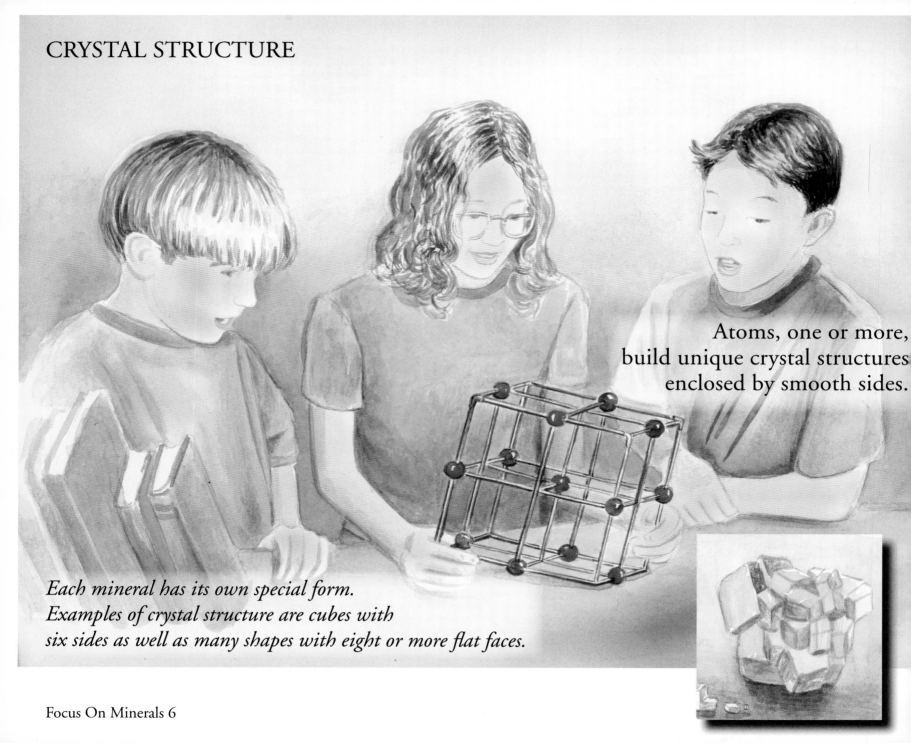

Atoms, one or more,
build unique crystal structures
enclosed by smooth sides.

Each mineral has its own special form.
Examples of crystal structure are cubes with
six sides as well as many shapes with eight or more flat faces.

Cubes of clear crystal,
one part sodium
and one part chlorine,
I taste like salt; I am salt.
Halite is my mineral name.

*Halite is a unique mineral
used as a food seasoning.
Other chloride
salts, like potassium,
are too bitter for the table.*

COLOR

Don't depend on it.
Quartz may be clear,
white, brown, rose or purple.
Fluorite may be
purple, blue, green or yellow.
No fair!

*Color may be exacting for certain minerals
but another property is generally
needed to support a correct identification.*

QUARTZ

Quartz crystals enjoy
wearing colors;
changing names:
pink of rose quartz,
purple of amethyst,
orange of citrine,
brown of smoky.

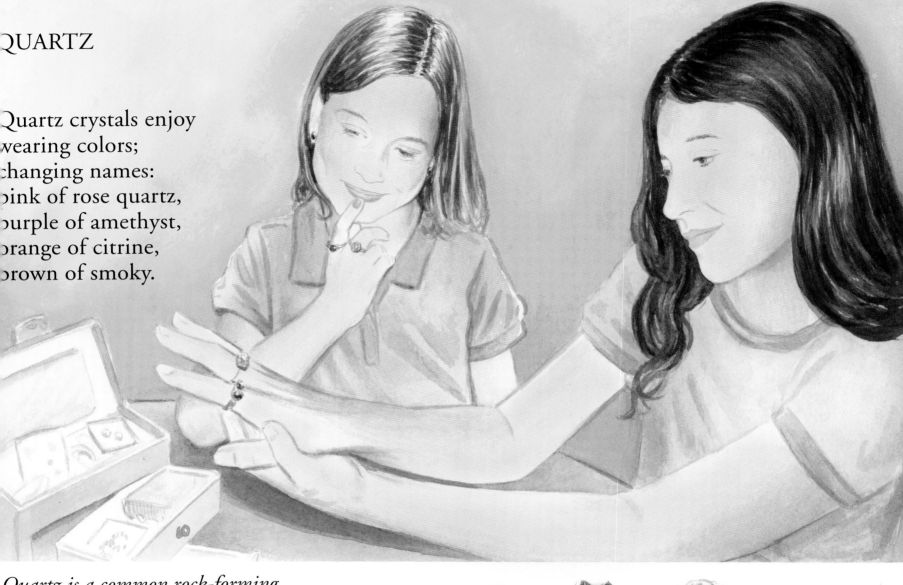

*Quartz is a common rock-forming
mineral and made of silica and oxygen;
the same elements are in window glass.*

9 Focus On Minerals

CORUNDUM GEMSTONES

Corundum,
when crystal clear,
blazes red off rubies,
glows blue off sapphires.
Jewels for crowns
on kings and queens.

Demanded by jewelers, gemstones are minerals found as crystals; the rarer the mineral the more it costs. In crystal form corundum looks like a barrel with six flat sides. It must be cut as a gemstone.

TURQUOISE

Pueblo tribes -
Anastazi, Acuma,
Zuni, Hopi, Navajo -
collected sky blue
heartstones,
sacred in ceremonies,
beautiful in jewelry,
valuable in trade.

Pueblo traders sold to
Blackfeet in the north,
Miwak and Chunash
on the west coast and
Cherokee in the east.
Today, they sell to
tourists in Southwestern
United States.

Lapis Lazuli
beautiful as it sounds,
an azure blue gemstone.

*Three minerals mix to form Lapis lazuli,
calcite, lazurite and pyrite. Lapis is called a gemstone,
not a gem. Lazurite is composed of the
elements sodium, aluminum, silica, oxygen and sulfur.*

MOVING COLORS

Turn an opal in your hand.
Colors change on demand,
fire opal red to yellow,
precious opal gray-blue-yellow.

Society has demanded opals since the times of the Pharaohs.
Opals are composed of the elements
silica and oxygen with attached water.

STREAK

Iron-oxide minerals
separate on streak alone;
magnetite black as charcoal,
hematite red as a fire truck,
limonite yellow brown like a dead leaf.

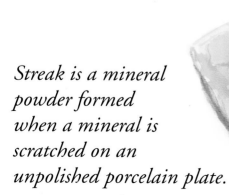

*Streak is a mineral
powder formed
when a mineral is
scratched on an
unpolished porcelain plate.*

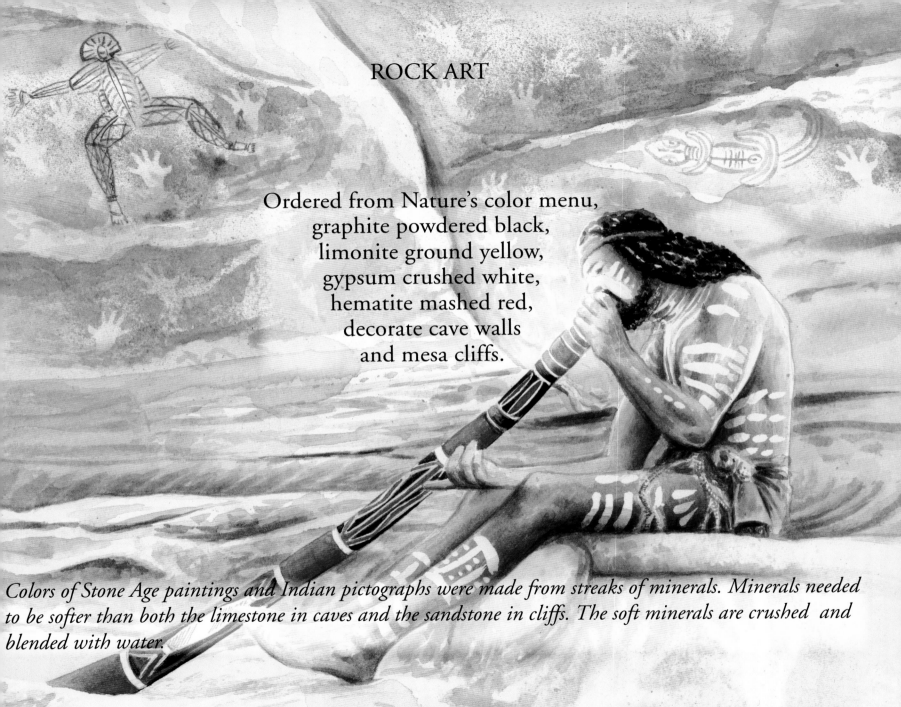

ROCK ART

Ordered from Nature's color menu,
graphite powdered black,
limonite ground yellow,
gypsum crushed white,
hematite mashed red,
decorate cave walls
and mesa cliffs.

Colors of Stone Age paintings and Indian pictographs were made from streaks of minerals. Minerals needed to be softer than both the limestone in caves and the sandstone in cliffs. The soft minerals are crushed and blended with water.

LUSTER

Galena gleams
a dull metallic.
Quartz glows
shiny, glassy, vitreous.
So easy to
tell apart.

*Luster refers to the surface
appearance of a mineral in
reflected light. Other examples
are adamantine diamond,
resinous sphalerite,
greasy jade and pearly talc.*

PYRITE

Yellow cubes faces
finely grooved hang out
on hard coal ledges,
glitter in the sun.
Fool's gold!

Pyrite is a cube shaped, metallic mineral made of iron and sulfur, often confused with gold by new mineral collectors.

HARDNESS

Important to know
the hardness
scale of Moh.
Scratch mineral
against mineral;
hardness wins.

From the softest to the
hardest, the relative scale is:
1. Talc, 2. Gypsum,
3. Calcite, 4. Fluorite, 5. Apatite,
6. Feldspar, 7. Quartz, 8. Topaz,
9. Corundum, 10. Diamond.
Friederich Moh, a German mineralogist,
developed his scale of hardness in 1822.
The scale still works well today for jewelers;
most precious gems are harder than 7.

TALC

Softest mineral
of them all, crushed to powder,
gives a glow to mother's skin;
soothes baby's bottom.

Stir talcum powder
with a finger feeling the
heavenly softness.

Pop a powder puff;
snowy clouds arise,
drifting in air.

Talc is the softest mineral, hardness of one;
its gray pearly luster feels slick to the touch.
Talc is composed of hydrogen, magnesium, silica and oxygen

ALABASTER

White to gray,
soft enough to
carve and sculpt,
texture confers
long lasting strength,
provides centuries
of endurance,
Bronze Age cultures
till today.

*Alabaster is a soft, fine-grained,
dense mineral form of Gypsum or Calcite.*

FREE FORM

On its pedestal
A selenite finger
Glowing silky white
Sags under its own weight
Bends a narcissistic bow
In admiration
Of its own beauty.

Selenite is a pure white, crystalline, sometimes fibrous form of Gypsum. Gypsum is a common rock-forming mineral, often associated with rock salt or limestone.

ABRASIVES

Smoothing.
Grinding.
Polishing.
Choose from Moh:
quartz in sand paper,
garnet in emery boards,
corundum-polishing steel,
diamond cuts all.

Abrasives are valuable minerals in industry. For example, diamonds are the teeth in oil-well-drilling bits able to slice through the hardest rock.

GALENA CLEAVAGE

Brightly metallic
as a new dime,
breaks into cube
after cube,
after cube,
smaller and
smaller,
until rice size.
Heavier than steel,
inside
among it's cubes,
bits of silver
hide a secret treasure.

Cleavage is the property of minerals breaking along planes into one shape again and again. Galena has three planes of cleavage. Galena, made of lead and sulfur, is the principal ore of lead and an important ore of silver. Ore minerals supply all the kinds of metals we use including iron, zinc, copper and many others.

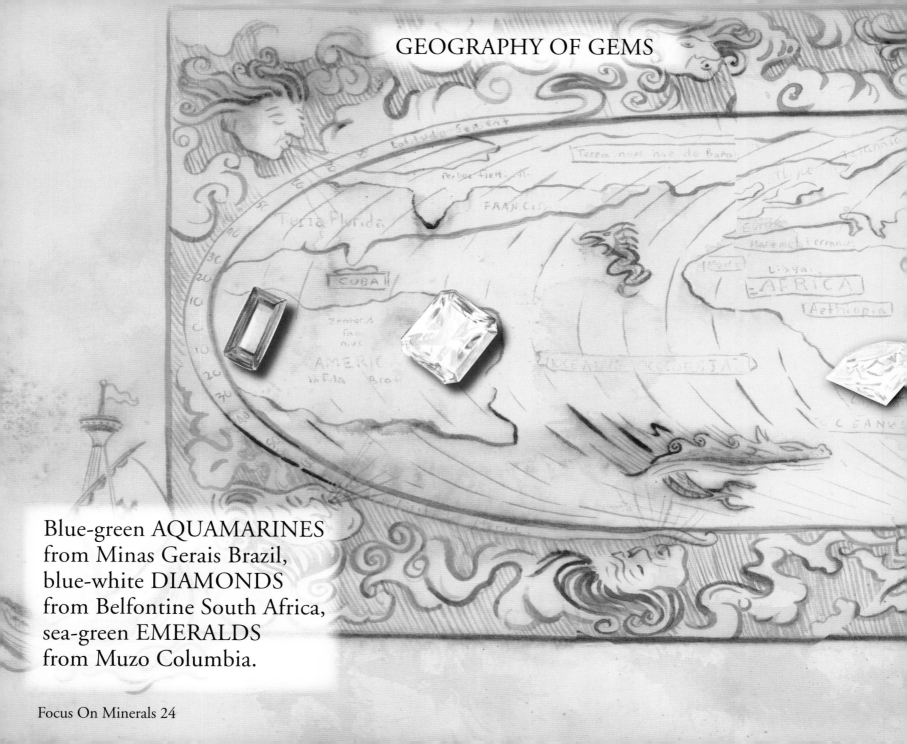

Blue-green AQUAMARINES
from Minas Gerais Brazil,
blue-white DIAMONDS
from Belfontine South Africa,
sea-green EMERALDS
from Muzo Columbia.

Deep-red RUBIES
from Mogok Myanmar,
indigo star SAPPHIRES
from Kashmir India
decorate Turkistan Turbans
for Ottoman Pashas.

*Precious gem minerals - found as clear crystals -
bring a valuable resource to these coutries.*

MUSCOVITE

Sheet after
sheet after
sheet
peels away,
translucent first
then transparent,
making windows
for ovens,
crushing into
make-believe
Christmas
Snow.

Muscovite belongs to the mica family; it is the only clear mica. Muscovite cleaves along one plane of cleavage, named basal cleavage, often called the most perfect cleavage of any mineral. Muscovite still is used as a window in very hot ovens, a good insulator. Its composition is complicated and includes potassium, aluminum, oxygen, hydrogen and silica.

REFRACTION

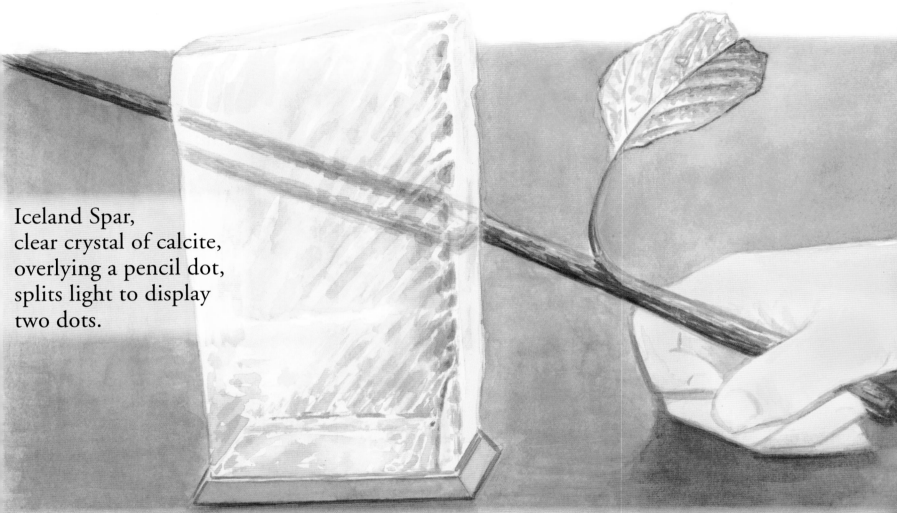

Iceland Spar,
clear crystal of calcite,
overlying a pencil dot,
splits light to display
two dots.

Each mineral has a distinct refraction property. Calcite, the principal element in limestone, is composed of calcium, carbon and oxygen. Calcite has three planes of cleavage at angles, forming rhombs.

ORNAMENTAL QUARTZ

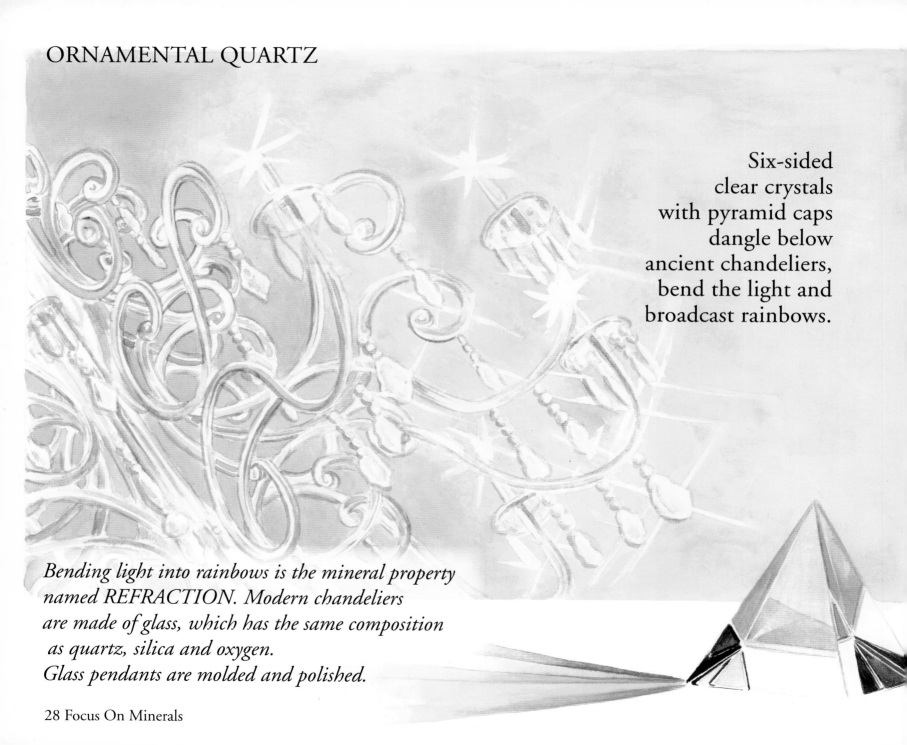

Six-sided
clear crystals
with pyramid caps
dangle below
ancient chandeliers,
bend the light and
broadcast rainbows.

Bending light into rainbows is the mineral property
named REFRACTION. Modern chandeliers
are made of glass, which has the same composition
as quartz, silica and oxygen.
Glass pendants are molded and polished.

MAGNETITE

Ebony fragments leap
onto a magnet, cling to
an open knife blade.

*A rock made wholly of magnetite is called
a "lodestone" because of its ability to
control the position of a compass needle.
It is the most magnetic mineral.
Magnetite is composed of the
elements iron and oxygen.*

DIMORPHISM

Made of pure carbon:
graphite so soft
it smudges paper,
diamond so hard
it cuts every single thing.

Dimorphism is a property of minerals in which minerals have the same composition but different crystal structure.

ELEMENTAL SULFUR

Scary!
Climbing into the volcanic crater.
Short of breath from altitude.
Scorched by rising heat.
Choking on the smell of rotten eggs.
Digging gorgeous sulfur crystals,
glazed vitreous yellow
midst kidney-shaped masses.
Earning the name Brimstone.

Only nine minerals occur as pure elements: sulfur, diamond and graphite as carbon, platinum, gold, silver, copper, arsenic and bismuth.

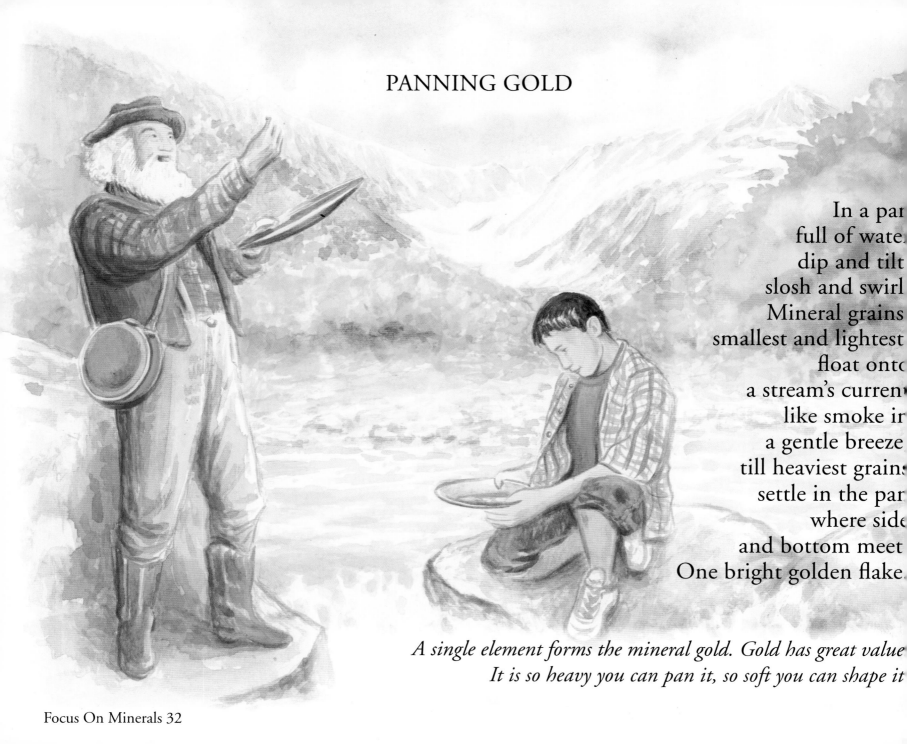

PANNING GOLD

In a pan
full of water
dip and tilt
slosh and swirl
Mineral grains
smallest and lightest
float onto
a stream's current
like smoke in
a gentle breeze
till heaviest grains
settle in the pan
where side
and bottom meet
One bright golden flake.

A single element forms the mineral gold. Gold has great value
It is so heavy you can pan it, so soft you can shape it

DOWNSIDE

Native gold
native silver
valued minerals
twisted hearts of man
bought weapons of warriors
tempted pirates and highwaymen
funded conquistadors
destroyed Inca and Aztec
stole their civilizations.

Pure gold and silver occur as native minerals made solely of a single element.

MINERAL AGES

The Stone Age ends.
Minerals of
tin and copper
melt out of rocks,
fall into a fire,
flowing together
create a metal
seen-never-before.

*Bronze is a metal alloy
of tin and copper.
Cassiterite, called tinstone,
is the principal mineral for tin.
Native copper or cuprite are
minerals that probably yielded
the first copper.*

Pre 3500 BC

The Bronze Age begins
a new age of
durable ornaments
bracelets and rings
vases and pots
and lasting statues.
Households grow handsomer.

3500 BC to 1000 BC

The Iron Age begin
a new tim
of strong, sharp
weapons
swords and daggers
spears and lances
shields and armor
Wars become deadlier

Post 1000 BC

IRON-OXIDE MINERALS

Magnetite, hematite, limonite
make Grandma's black skillet,
Mom's steel pans.

*These three ore minerals are composed
of iron and oxygen in different
proportions. They have long history
in producing iron and steel.*

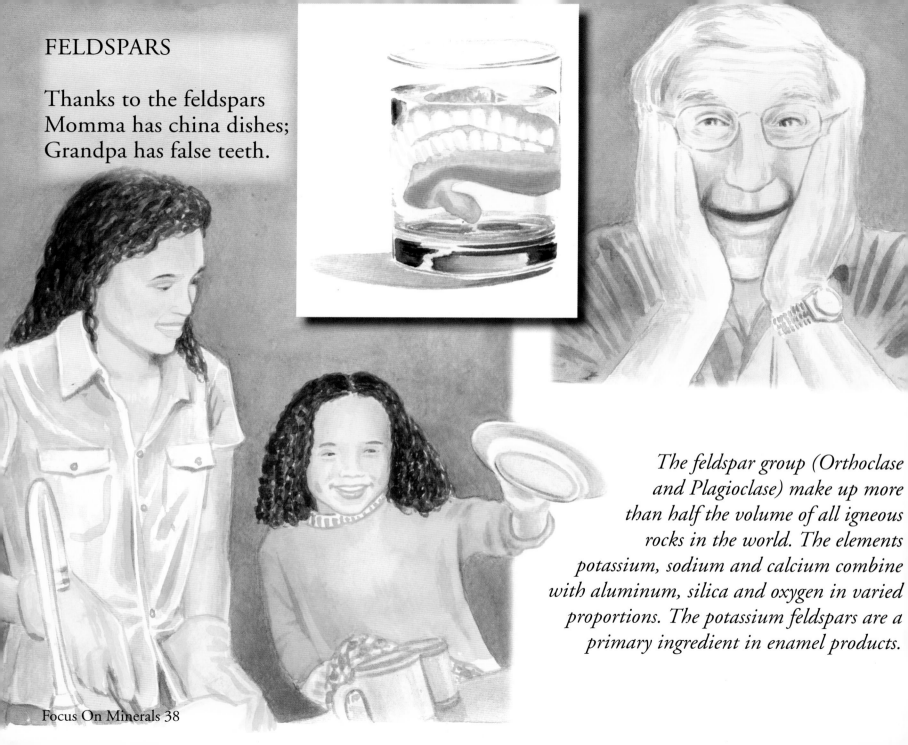

FELDSPARS

Thanks to the feldspars
Momma has china dishes;
Grandpa has false teeth.

The feldspar group (Orthoclase and Plagioclase) make up more than half the volume of all igneous rocks in the world. The elements potassium, sodium and calcium combine with aluminum, silica and oxygen in varied proportions. The potassium feldspars are a primary ingredient in enamel products.

BIRTHSTONES

Give a bloodstone
brooch to a Pisces,
an emerald earring to a Taurus,
a pearl pendant to a Gemini,
a ruby ring to a Cancer,
a topaz tiara for a Scorpio.

BIRTHSTONES are gems and gemstones assigned to each month. Find your birthstone: Garnet for January, Amethyst for February, Bloodstone for March, Diamond for April, Emerald for May, Pearl for June, Ruby for July, Onyx or Peridot for August, Sapphire for September, Opal for October, Topaz for November, Turquoise for December.

THE STONE CARVER

Fingers quivered,
twitched and trembled
seeking to caress
the block of Jade.
Images of lustrous
rings and necklaces,
vases and bowls,
statues and figures,
floated and hovered
behind her eyes.

Jade is a family name for varieties of the minerals Jadeite and Nephrite.
They occur in many different colors. Many famous carvings from Mexico and China are jade.

AGATE

Micro-size quartz crystals
in brilliant colors
band together
around geode rims,
in layers replacing wood,
as grapelike masses
surrounding springs.

Chalcedony is the inclusive term for banded microcrystalline quartz deposited by water moving through fine pores in rock or wood. Chalcedony gemstones are agate and onyx.

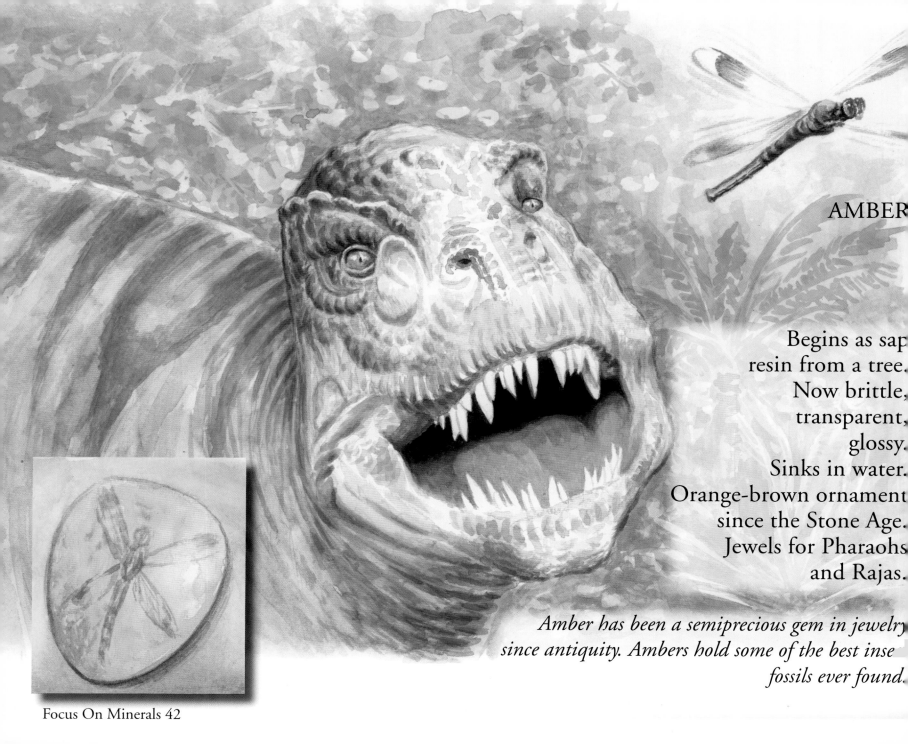

AMBER

Begins as sap,
resin from a tree.
Now brittle,
transparent,
glossy.
Sinks in water.
Orange-brown ornament
since the Stone Age.
Jewels for Pharaohs
and Rajas.

Amber has been a semiprecious gem in jewelry
since antiquity. Ambers hold some of the best inse
fossils ever found.

Focus On Minerals 42

BAUXITE

Bauxite from Guiana,
shipped in monster freighters,
covered by rusty red dust,
unloaded to electric smelters,
separated from a muddy bath,
produces bright shiny aluminum.

*Bauxite, an oxide of aluminum, has an earthy structure like limonite;
neither has a known crystal structure.*

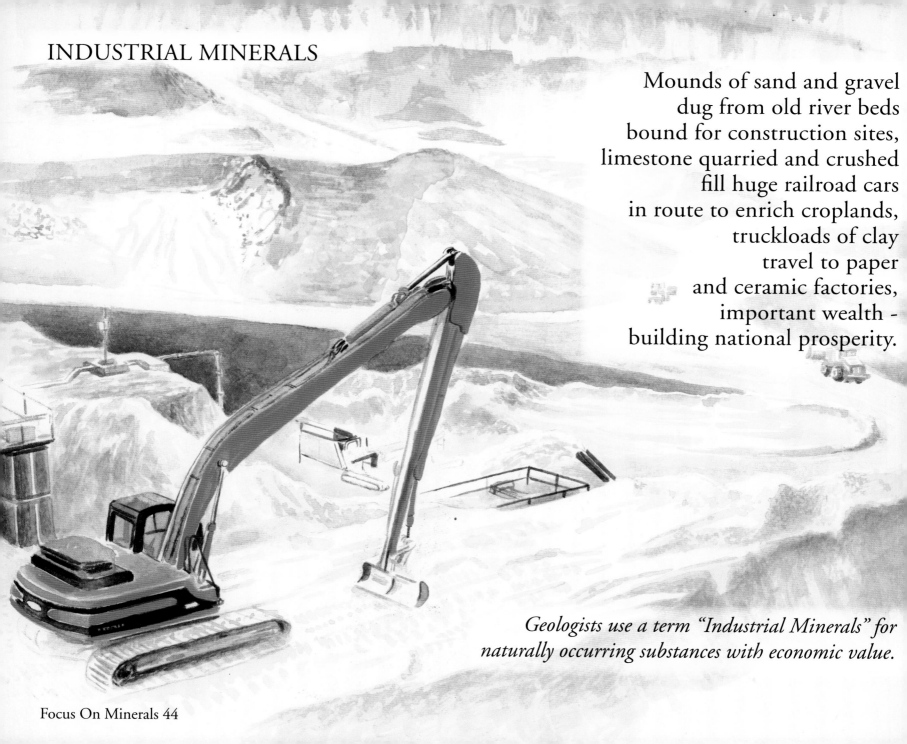

INDUSTRIAL MINERALS

Mounds of sand and gravel
dug from old river beds
bound for construction sites,
limestone quarried and crushed
fill huge railroad cars
in route to enrich croplands,
truckloads of clay
travel to paper
and ceramic factories,
important wealth -
building national prosperity.

*Geologists use a term "Industrial Minerals" for
naturally occurring substances with economic value.*

SHOWTIME

If nearby, you must go to a gem and mineral show!

At a gem and mineral show, you see inexpensive specimens, readily purchased, as well as exotic specimens that cost a lot. It is like visiting a museum.

Focus on Minerals Glossary

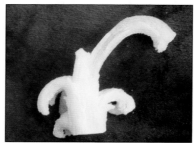

TALC: $H_2Mg_3Si_4O_{12}$ gray-green crystals flaky or splintery soft scratches with finger nail, pearly luster feels soapy.

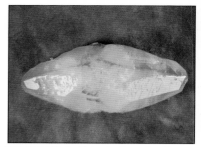

GYPSUM: $CaSO_4-2H_2O$ Selenite crystals like arrowheads, dense, translucent to opaque, (H2) soft scratches with finger nail, often iron stained.

CALCITE: $CaCO_3$ six-sided pointed crystals, white to brown, (H3) scratches with penny, rhombic cleavage, when clear shows double refraction.

FLUORITE: CaF_2 cubic, glassy, varicolored often purple, (H4), four cleavages make eight-sided crystals.

APATITE: $Ca_2F(PO)_3$ tabular glossy yellow-brown, (H5), prismatic, round edges.

FELDSPAR: CaorNaorKAlSiO8 tabular, white to tan, (H6), brittle, three cleavages. Blocky.

QUARTZ: SiO_2 hexagonal, prismatic, glassy, varicolored, (H7), brittle, fractures into concave forms shaped like inside of a shell.

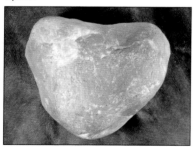

TOPAZ: $Al_2(F,OH)SiO_4$ tabular to granular, glassy, yellow-blue, one cleavage plane, medium heavy.

CORUNDUM: Al_2O_3 hexagonal, prismatic, barrel shaped, varicolored, often brown to pink, (9), medium heavy.

RUBY: deep red, crystalline, precious gem, form of Corundum.

SAPPHIRE: transparent, blue, crystalline, precious gem of Corundum.

DIAMOND: C cubic, found as crystals or crystal fragments, glassy, (H10), four cleavage planes, found in weathered blue igneous rock or in alluvium.

GRAPHITE: C hexagonal, opaque, dark gray, black streak, (H1), marks paper, platy, feels greasy, light weight.

SULFUR: S pyramidal, resinous, distinctive yellow, (H2.2), uneven fracture, can be fibrous or granular, light weight.

GOLD: Au cubic, distorted crystals, opaque, distinctive gold color, metallic, can be shaped, sometimes flaky, very heavy.

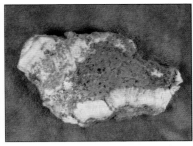

SILVER: Ag cubic, crystals usually small, wiry, hairy, platy, silver-white to gray-black, metallic, can be shaped into wire, heavy.

COPPER: Cu cubic, distorted crystals, scaly to massive, hackly fracture, copper red, heavy.

HALITE: NaCl cubic, colorless or white , glassy, (H2), tastes like salt, gathers moisture.

SPHALERITE: ZnS 12-sided crystal, rounded, fibrous, grapelike, brown, brownish streak, submetallic greasy luster, medium weight.

GALENA: PbS cubic, dark gray, metallic, cubic cleavage, heavy.

PYRITE: FeS cubic, striated faces, golden yellow, "fool's gold," metallic, brittle, when granular may have rusty spots.

MAGNETITE: Fe304 cubic, striated, black, metallic, brittle, medium heavy, magnetic.

HEMATITE: Fe2O3 hexagonal, scaly, fine granular, gray to red, metallic to earthy, red streak, moderate weight.

LIMONITE: Fe2O3-nH2O massive, earthy, clay like, brownish yellow color and streak, sometimes gritty, found in bogs and swamps.

BAUXITE: Al23 noncrytalline, clusters of rounded beads, earthy, yellow brown to red, soft, clay smell, light weight.

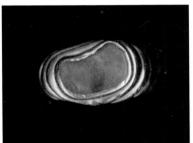

OPAL: SiO2-nH2O amorphous, irregular masses, glassy, varicolored, light weight, greasy luster, (H6), often beautiful play of colors.

LAPIS: (Lazurrite) 3NaAlSiO4.Na2S cubic, crystals rare, deep azure blue, glassy, light weight.

URQUOISE: H5[Al(OH)2]Cu(OH)(PO4)4 tabular are, usually amorphous, shades of blue or green, waxy to dull, (H6), light weight.

JADE: Ca(Mg,Fe)(OH)2(Si4O11)2 compact, granular, varicolored dark green to white, greasy luster, (H2), brittle fracture, readily carved.

BERYL: Be3Al2Si6O18 hexagonal, elongate, prismatic, various-green colored, (H 7.5-8), Beryllium ore.

AQUAMARINE: long transparent prisms blue to sea green, gemstone variety of Beryl.

EMERALD: crystalline, transparent emerald green, precious gem, variety of Beryl.

AMBER: C10H16O fossil resin, transparent to milky, honey colored, orange yellow brown, semi precious gem, often contains fossil insects.

MUSCOVITE: KAl2(OH)2AlSi3)10 tabular, hexagonal, brownish large booklike crystals, pearly luster, H2-3, cleaves into sheets along one plane.

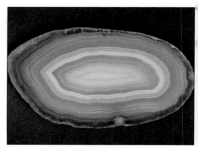

AGATE or CHALCEDONY: SiO2, compact, microcrystalline, translucent to transparent, banded and clouded, multicolored, commonly rims geodes.

Terms

Geode. A hollow, more or less globular rock with an outer layer of dense banded chalcedony with inward projecting crystals.

Prismatic and/or Pyramidal. A crystal with a pointed end having three to twelve faces.

Striated. Parallel line of grooves mark a crystal surface.

Tabular. A crystal form in which two dimensions are larger than the third; faces often parallel.

Adamanite. Refers to a brilliant luster like that of a well cut pure diamond.

Hexagonal. Refers to a crystal shape with six sides enclosing the long dimension.

Microcrystaline. A texture of a mineral or a rock consisting of minute crystals only visible under a microscope.

Smelter. A place where metallic ore minerals are crushed, ground, melted or fused to separate metal from impurities.

Minerals

Ag Silver
Al Aluminum
Au Gold
Be Beryllium
C Carbon
Ca Calcium
Cl Chlorine
Cu Copper
F Fluorine
Fe Iron
H Hydrogen
K Potassium
Mg Magnesium
Na Sodium
O Oxygen
P Phosphorous
Pb Lead
S Sulfur
Si Silica
Zn Zinc